RAF COSFORD

ALEC BREW

The History Press

Arriving at RAF Cosford the hard way: a member of the RAF Falcons Parachute Display Team leaving a Hercules. Cosford's runway begins just by his right toe, and his left knee is over the centre of Albrighton. The M54 motorway just behind his head is a more normal way to visit Cosford.

First published in 1995
This edition published 2009

The History Press
The Mill, Brimscombe Port
Stroud, Gloucestershire, GL5 2QG
www.thehistorypress.co.uk

British Library Cataloguing in Publication Data.
A catalogue record for this book is available from the British Library.

ISBN 978 0 7524 5211 1

Typesetting and origination by The History Press
Printed in Great Britain

Contents

Bristol Britannia 312F, G-AOVF, in the colours of BOAC, part of the British Airways airliner collection held at the Aerospace Museum, Cosford.

Introduction

RAF Cosford is a quiet but vitally important part of the Royal Air Force. It is not a famous operational station like Manston, Scampton, Tangmere or others, it has always been a training base for ground-based trades, and yet perversely its name is probably better known because of its Indoor Athletics Arena and Aerospace Museum.

Since its opening in August 1938 RAF Cosford has trained tens of thousands of RAF technicians, a number increasing annually as Cosford becomes, with the closure of Halton, the sole such training base.

Although the station only opened in 1938, having been built as the home of No. 2 School of Technical Training, flying had actually come to Cosford three years earlier. Alan Cobham brought his National Aviation Day Display to Cosford on 6 September 1935. They flew from a field on the other side of the Shifnal road from the later airfield, at the bottom of Kennel Bank, and the star of the show was a Flying Flea. How appropriate that an example of Henri Mignet's little home-built aircraft, beautifully restored, is now on display in the Aerospace Museum.

One wing of apprentices moved by train from Halton between 18 and 29 July 1938 to form the nucleus of No. 2 SoTT. Apart from personnel the move included 22 instructional aircraft, 179 half-ton workbenches, 800 fitters' vices and 1,333 tool-boxes and kits.

In March 1939 No. 9 Maintenance Unit moved into the first of the large C-type hangars to be completed, and was to be the other main resident unit at Cosford, storing and preparing aircraft for RAF service.

The C-type hangars were augmented with a clutch of turf-covered Lamella hangars on the other side of the airfield, a row of Bellman hangars by the railway station, and during the war some small Robin hangars scattered about as far afield as Beckbury. The airfield itself was originally all grass, but a paved runway was built in 1941.

No. 9 MU was heavily involved with preparing Spitfires from Castle Bromwich, and later, in April 1942, Horsa gliders, a tug and glider flight were being formed. Such was the congestion at 9 MU that two satellite landing grounds were built, at Brocton and Weston Park. Ferrying aircraft was the responsibility of No. 12 Ferry Pilots' Pool, which in 1943 became the first all-women pool, commanded by Mrs Marion Wilberforce.

No. 2 School of Technical Training trained over 70,000 engine and airframe mechanics and armourers during the war; from 1939 to 1942 Cosford was one of three Officer Training Schools for ground-based trades, which amalgamated at Cosford in 1943 as the Officer Cadet Training Unit, remaining there until 1948.

Another famous Cosford institution, the RAF Hospital, opened in 1940, with 503 beds, a Burns Unit following in 1941. Over 42,000 patients were treated during the war, and during peacetime the hospital was also open to the local civilian population (including myself on one occasion) until its closure in 1977.

After the war No. 2 SoTT formally reverted from adult to youth training in 1950, and by 1953 there were 2,500 boy entrants on eighteen-month training courses. In more recent times apprentice training has been replaced by direct entry adult trade training.

The RAF School of Photography moved to Cosford in 1963 and now trains photographers of all three services. The RAF School of Physical Training returned to Cosford in 1977 having left twenty-three years earlier.

Until fairly recently Cosford was the only available venue for AAA National Indoor Athletics Championships, and International Indoor Athletic matches. It is for this reason, more than any other, that people all over the country, if not the world, scurry to try and find Cosford on the map, one of those sporting places, like Silverstone and Badminton, which are known to everyone without necessarily knowing where they are.

Since the war the airfield at Cosford has been one of the quietest in the RAF. No. 9 MU disbanded in 1959 to be replaced by 236 MU, responsible for motor transport, and the most familiar flying has been the gliders of No. 633 Air Cadet Gliding School and the Wrekin Gliding Club. From 1978 Cosford has also been home to the University of Birmingham Air Squadron.

The exception, noise-wise, has been the annual air display, which has attracted hundreds of thousands of people over the years, and continues to do so. My own visits from the age of ten, and I am sure those of many other people, have inspired a lifelong interest in aviation.

Visitors to the air displays have always been able to see a fine collection of vintage aircraft at Cosford. The collection has now been hugely expanded as the RAF Museum Cosford, officially part of the overall RAF Museum, and even larger in size than the main museum at Hendon. The British Airways collection of jet airliners which had been a feature of Cosford for many years was disposed of in 2005, but in 2006 the iconic new building housing the Cold War Museum opened. Over the following two years more than 600,000 people visited.

Reflecting the multi service nature of the trainees at Cosford, the station has now been renamed The Defence College of Aeronautical Engineering Cosford, or DCAE Cosford. In the minds of local people it remains RAF Cosford however, and is destined to remain an integral part of the local community even if the training function is lost to a proposed new aeronautical college at St Athan.

One

CONSTRUCTION

*In April 1938 preparations for war were being
made in a quiet corner of Shropshire.*

RAF Cosford was the first major contract won by Sir Alfred McAlpine & Son Ltd, after Alfred had broken away from the family firm of Sir Robert McAlpine in 1936 to form his own construction company with a head office in the Wirral. Their tender was only £700 less than the next lowest, and those few pounds were to be very important in the history of the company, setting it on the road to becoming one of the country's major contractors, and establishing it in Wolverhampton. A Southern Region was set up with its offices initially at Cosford, but when the RAF required the office space new offices were found in Waterloo Road, Wolverhampton. Alfred McAlpine Ltd, as it later became, moved for a long while to Wergs Hall, but was taken over by Carillion, another local company, in 2007.

A Lamella concrete storage hangar under construction at Cosford in 1938. The concrete roof was poured in sections and, when finished, was covered in turf to camouflage it. The shape was such that it left no tell-tale shadows.

One of the large D-type hangars under construction in October 1938. A railway track was laid on each side of the hangar to carry the large steam-powered cranes, or 'navvies'.

The formwork for the first section of a Lamella hangar. The massive wooden sections were moved along bay by bay, and then from hangar to hangar.

Just to show everything did not go entirely to plan, the formwork tower on the right of this D-type hangar has toppled over.

A D-type hangar nearing completion. A curved row of these was built on the north side of the airfield.

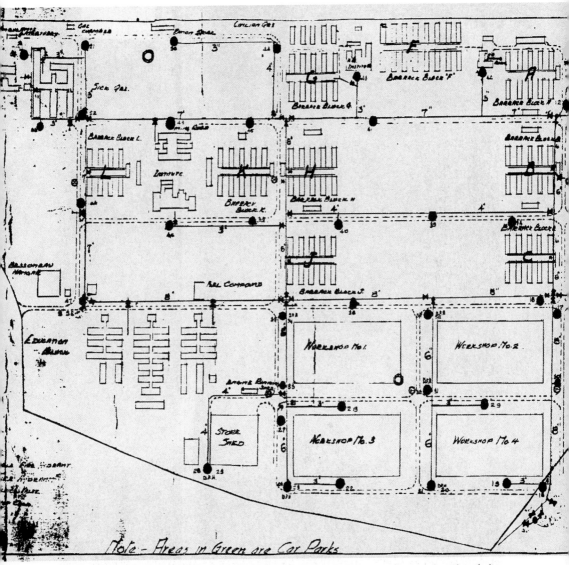

A construction drawing showing Cosford's main buildings on the north side of the railway, the airfield being to the south. Workshop No. 4 has now become the Indoor Athletics Arena. Many of the wooden barrack blocks have long since been replaced, although some are still in use.

Fulton Block nearly complete. A Health & Safety Inspector today would close the site immediately as there are no handrails around the roof. Note the workman on the edge of the left-hand block.

The progress of a Lamella hangar under construction. The first bay has been concreted, formwork is in place for the second bay, which is probably being poured, and a formwork tower is already in position for the next bay.

The near completion of a Lamella roof, with waterproofing having just started. Note the steamroller.

A virtually complete Lamella, with turf being applied to the roof. The photograph was taken from an already completed Lamella on 4 August 1939. The Second World War was only a month away.

The completed Fulton Block which was named after Captain John Fulton of the Royal Engineers, who was one of the founding fathers of the Royal Flying Corps.

Two

RAF TRAINING

Learning the technical skills to keep the RAF flying.

RAF Cosford has only ever been a training base, the home of No. 2 School of Technical Training and a number of other training institutions, which currently include the Joint School of Photography and the RAF School of Physical Training. The most common aircraft in the skies over Cosford have been the gliders and tug aircraft of the ATC Air Experience Squadron and the Wrekin Gliding Club, and the Chipmunks and Bulldogs of the University of Birmingham Air Squadron. Cosford is destined to remain a RAF training base into the next century, one of the few RAF airfields where major construction is taking place, in some cases to replace the 'temporary' wooden huts which were erected nearly sixty years ago. With the closure of RAF Halton, Cosford was 'promoted' to No.1 School of Technical Training, but in 2004 became the Defence College of Aeronautical Engineering, reflecting its new multi-service role.

Apprentices under instruction on a Hawker Hart biplane. The numbers of them would seem to indicate a shortage of airframes for instructional purposes.

The thirty-sixth entry of Halton apprentices photographed at Halton (No. 1 School of Technical Training) prior to their departure for Cosford to complete their training.

The RAF Cosford Band, 1939. Far right on the back row is Harry Pointon, who was a cook and later a sergeant. He died in October 1942 in Abadan, when his tent caught fire.

A group of apprentices in 1940 being shown how to swing a propeller, on a camouflaged De Havilland Gipsy Moth, probably an impressed civil machine. In the background are two Hawker Harts, one without its wings.

The Station Boxing Team, 1939. Back row, left to right: CAA Nichol, AA Harris, AA Griffiths, AA Alexander, AA Arnold, Sgt. MacLean. Middle row: AC Lewis, LAA Lewis, LAA Tubbs-Merrick, AC Alison, LAA Smith, LAA Hawes, Sgt. Morris. Front row: LAC Butler, Flg. Off. Jenkins, Gp. Capt. W.J.Y. Guilfoyle OBE, MC, WO Hole, AA Humphreys.

The Apprentice Gymnastics Team, summer term 1939. Back row, left to right: Cpl. Barker, AA Clinton, LAA Goffey, AA Ashby, AA Colclough, AA Shaw, AA Kirk. Front row: AA Ethell, LAA Markey, WO Hole, AA Eggo, LAA Stott.

Part of the Apprentices' Pipe and Drum Band, October 1939.

Cosford's first 'Passing Out' Parade on 25 July 1939, with part of the 1936 entry marching past.

On 13 February 1941 Boulton Paul Defiant N3518 stalled on approach to Cosford, on a ferry flight from Pendeford for storage, and crashed. The aircraft was repaired and later served with No. 410 Squadron and No. 10 Air Gunnery School. It was eventually struck off charge on 8 July 1943, with 270.25 flying hours.

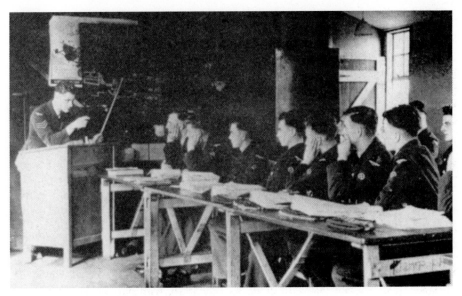

A classroom of apprentices under instruction.

The 'Passing Out' Parade, February 1940.

No. 1 (A) Wing Junior Athletics Team (winners of the Inter-wing Championship in 1939). Back row, left to right: Waugh, Leach, Draper, Saban, Jones, Holt, Reeve, Shipman, Stockford, Brooker, Semple. Middle row: Cpl. Cockcroft, Cox, Brigginshaw, Owens, Gurr, Morris, Parker, Lewis, Smith, Neill, Cpl. Dale, Flg.Sgt. E. Barnes. Front row: Tofts, Flg.Sgt. Bollins, Flg.Lt. W. Anderson, Wg.Cdr. K.A. Meek OBE, WO Franklin, Sgt Edwards, Knight.

Cosford's Birmingham League Football Team for the season 1940–41, including many
Football League players. Back row, left to right: Sgt. O'Donnell (Aston Villa), Sgt. Smith
(Chelsea), Sgt. Bert Williams (Walsall, and after the war of Wolves and England), AC
Young (Huddersfield), Cpl. Acquana (Hull). Front row: Cpl. Sims (Wellington), AC
Farell (Brighton & Hove Albion), Staaley, Sgt. Hill (Blackpool), Cpl. Hill (Dulwich
Hamlet), Sgt. Newman (Walsall).

Cosford's Wolverhampton League Team, champions in the season 1940–41. Back row,
left to right: Sgt. Roberts (Colwyn Bay), Sgt. Donaldson (Falkirk), LAC Evans (Sheffield
Wednesday), AC Fowler (Leeds), LAC Mitton (Wolves), Flt.Lt. G. Thorpe (England
Rugby International). Front row: Cpl. Williams, Flt.Sgt. Aldridge (Captain), Sgt. Turner,
Fl.Sgt. Lewis, AC Jack.

Czech airmen on parade at Cosford, August 1940. Most are wearing RAF uniforms. From August to December 1940 Cosford was home to the Czech Depot, for the testing and training of Czech officers and airmen who had escaped the German occupation, often after a period in France.

A Handley Page Halifax fitted with a Boulton Paul Type D Turret with twin 0.5 in. machine-guns and radar control, February 1944. A number of Wellingtons can be seen in the background.

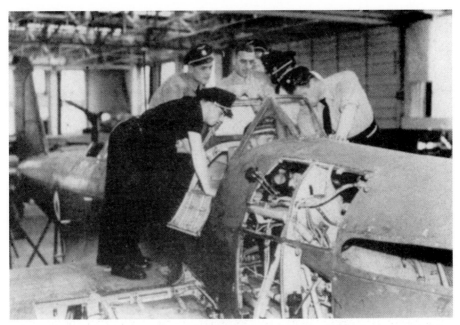

Czech airmen learning the ins and outs of the Fairey Battle. Most were posted to the four dedicated Czech squadrons in the RAF, Nos 310–313.

A group of Czech pilots at Cosford, August 1940. These pilots had all flown with the French Air Force after escaping the German occupation of their homeland, and then had to escape for a second time.

The RAF and Czech officers in charge of the Czech Depot.

Czech airmen working on a nine-cylinder radial engine. Though many of them were experienced fitters, they nevertheless had to become acquainted with British equipment.

On 19 April 1940 King George VI and Queen Elizabeth (The Queen Mother as she is now) visited RAF Cosford. Here the Queen is showing a keen interest in the needle used for sewing fabric on a wing.

The Queen is talking to an airman who appears to be sewing fabric on an aileron.

A much later Royal visitor to Cosford. Prince Bernhard of the Netherlands is talking to the Station Commander, Group Captain Campbell in 1980. The Dutch have a strong link with the area as, during the War, the Prince Irene Brigade of the Dutch Army was housed at Wrottesley Park, a little way further south on the A41, and many Dutch soldiers married local girls and stayed in the area after the War.

Another Royal visitor, the Duke of Gloucester, visiting the Aerospace Museum in 1981. On his left is the Museum curator, Derek Eastwood, showing him a replica of the Moon Buggy.

A 'Passing Out' Parade in 1941 for members of the WAAFs who were also trained at Cosford.

The funeral of Apprentice Francis Patrick Eddy of Torquay at Donington Church, 1939. This was one of two funerals from Cosford in the same week, the other being for Apprentice James West of No. 3 Wing.

RAF Cosford operating theatre staff, 1940. Back row, left to right: Sgt. Walters (ORA), S/L Ross (Orthopaedic Surgeon), S/L Vere-Hodge (Orthopaedic Surgeon), S/L Anson (Anaesthetist), Cpl. Gray (ORA), LAC Nicholson, LAC Owens. Front row: -?- (Theatre Sister), Snr. Theatre Sister Brightman, -?- (Theatre Sister).

RAF Cosford staff outside the operating theatre, 1940. Left to right: Cpl. Hawkins, Cpl. Gray, Cpl. Williams, -?- (AC2), Cpl. Barry.

In the grounds outside the operating theatre of RAF Cosford Hospital, 1940. Left to right: Cpl. Gray (ORA), -?- (Sister), Sgt. Greening (ORA), Snr. Sister Maltman, LAC Owens (U/T ORA).

In the grounds of the hospital, 1941. In the background is the Inflammable Liquids Store used by the Dispensing Department. Left to right: -?- (LAC), LAC Owens, Sgt. Gray, LAC Nicholson, Cpl. Davies, with LAC Axon in front on the ground.

Another group of hospital staff, 1941. Back row, left to right: Sgt. Gray, LAC Nicholson, LAC Owens, -?-, Cpl. Davies, LAC Axon. Front row: -?- (Sister), Sister Moore, F.O. Calendar (CO and Anaesthetist), -?- (Sister), -?- (VAD Nurse).

WAAF recruits undergoing training at Cosford, 1941.

A Boulton Paul Type D Turret with radar scanner in the tail of a Halifax, 12 February 1944. Under the starboard wing is a Hawker Henley target tug, and under the port wing a Mosquito.

Physical jerks: PT for the apprentices during 1940. At least they are in one of the workshop buildings and therefore protected from the weather.

An early model Halifax Mk. 1 at Cosford as an instructional airframe, 1946. It carried the instructional serial 3690M.

The recruits of Hut F10, July 1951. Back row, left to right: Keith Castle (Nottingham), Allsop (Nottingham), -?-, -?-, Turner (Derby), Barnacle (Yorks.), Adams (Birmingham), -?- (Yorks.), Roy Ashby (London), -?- (Nottingham). Front row: Cocker (Scotland), Collins (London), Gupry (Lewisham), -?-, Clark (London), Sgt. Mills, (origin unknown) Cpl. Dicker (Brighton), Cheney (Leicester), Butterworth (Yorks.), Collins (London), Bartlett (Egham), Evans (Snr. Man., ex-ATC Birmingham).

An Avro Shackleton MR.1 used for ground instructional purposes at Cosford, in the early 1960s.

Air Commodore R.J.
Rodwell CB, RAF Station
Commander in 1951.

De Havilland Chipmunk WG483, of the Station Flight, about to land on a snowy runway, February 1964. This picture could have been taken during any winter from the early fifties to the present day.

Inside the Station Flight hangar, July 1961. A Cadet Mk. III, WT903, is being re-rigged after an airworthiness check. There is a Chipmunk in the foreground, and also visible are T31s XE807 and WT870, and T21s WB926 and WB946.

Slingsby T24 Falcon 4, VM109, operated by the Western Area Gliding Club at Cosford from March 1953.

The launch of Sedbergh T21b, WB946, January 1961.

A view of the two hangars, alongside the entrance road to the Aerospace Museum and the railway line, photographed from the T21b, WB946, from about 700 ft on 11 March 1961.

A single seat Slingsby Skylark having made a heavy landing and broken its back in the early 1960s.

The view from the same aircraft at about the same position; note the curve of the two windscreens on the T21b. There are two Air Experience Flight Avro Ansons just ahead, on and by the taxiway, and beyond them a number of goal-posts on the airfield.

Probably the same Skylark as on the previous page, landing behind a T.21 Sedburgh, before its unfortunate accident.

A T21b at the launch point at the western end of the airfield, with P.O. Crump (CFI) and F.O. Brown (Instructor).

The instructional airframe of the Hawker Hunter F6 parked out in the fresh air during a Battle of Britain Display.

Another instructional airframe is this Vickers Valetta T Mk. 3 navigational trainer. It is distinguishable from the transport version by the row of astrodomes along the roof.

A Handley Page Victor B1 in use as an instructional airframe in the 1960s. For a long while there were several V-bombers filling Cosford's hangars.

Not the result of a serious air crash, but the simulation of one. A Handley Page Hastings, TG554, cut up for crash rescue training in the 1960s. It was sited near the western boundary of the airfield.

Parade ground guardian at Cosford for many years, the Spitfire FR.XIVE, MT847, is now part of the Aerospace Museum collection, happily tucked up in a hangar in its own sandbag revetment.

A much later Handley Page Victor, a B.1A, XH592, which moved from instructional use at Cosford, to outside display at the Aerospace Museum for many years. Heavily corroded it was eventually scrapped when replaced by one of the retiring Victor K.2 tankers. This nose section was preserved at Bruntingthorpe.

The Goodyear airship *Europa* was a visitor to Cosford on several occasions, often giving flights to Goodyear employees and guests. On the first occasion members of the Wolverhampton Aero Club flew over from Pendeford Airport to watch what was then a novel sight, the first time an airship had been seen in the West Midlands since the Graf Zeppelin flew over the very same spot, following the railway line, in the 1930s.

Jet Provost T.4, XN499, being resprayed by the apprentices.

A Sepecat Jaguar, one of the most numerous airframes currently in use for instructional purposes at Cosford, June 1986.

A De Havilland Chipmunk of No. 8 Air Experience Flight outside one of the Bellman hangars.

A Slingsby Venture T2 motor glider, XZ554, used by No. 633 Air Cadet Gliding School. The school was founded in 1948 and draws Air Cadets from an area stretching from Warwick to Stafford, Oswestry to Worcester.

Bulldogs of the University of Birmingham Air Squadron taxi out. The squadron also gives flying training to students from the universities of Keele, Aston and Warwick.

The Spitfire's successor as parade-ground ornament was this Vampire T11. It, in turn, has been succeeded by a Hawker Hunter 6, serial XG225, outside the HQ building.

Jet Provost T.Mk.5A, XW311, one of many used extensively for ground handling training, out of over forty No. JP 5s retired to Cosford as instructional airframes.

The Bolkow Bo105 Air Ambulance helicopter, G-ABTHV, operated by Bond Helicopters from RAF Cosford, a service funded entirely by public donations. The service is estimated to save a life every month. This helicopter has since been replaced by a newer example.

De Havilland
Dominie, XS734,
one of six taken
on charge, for
instructional
purposes, after
serving at RAF
Cranwell, No. 3 FTS
and No. 6 FTS.

The Museum of the Joint School of Photography pictured in 1983 with its curator Jack Eggleston. The museum records the oldest school of technical training in the RAF, its origins going back to 1912, though it only arrived at Cosford in 1963.

Cosford station, which affords a fine view of RAF Cosford, situated as it is on an embankment in the centre of the base; the first and last view countless trainees have had of Cosford over many years.

Trainees at work on an ex-Red Arrows Folland Gnat in 1981. Compare this with the first picture in this section on page 20; both pictures feature two-seat aircraft from the Hawker-Siddeley stable, but in only forty-five years almost everything else has changed.

A restored example of an ATC Slingsby Cadet TX.3, XE799, owned by Vaughan Meers of the Staffordshire Aircraft Restoration Team, and on display at the 2007 Air Show, with the new gliding club hangar, which replaced the wartime Bellman hangars, in the background.

A Slingsgby Cadet TX.3, G-BPIP, which has been converted to a single seat Motor-Cadet, and owned by Bob Arnold and Vaughan Meers of the Staffordshire Aircraft Restoration Team, also at the 2007 Air Show.

A modern interpretation of the previous two concepts, a Grob 109B Vigilant T.1 motor-glider, the current ATC aerial carriage.

The cockpit of an ex-RAF instructional airframe, Hawker Hunter FGA.9, XE597 (Instructional serial 8874M), now privately owned by members of the Wolverhampton Aviation Group. Part of a huge new trend in private cockpit collecting, this was displayed at the 2007 Air Show.

Three

NO. 9 MU

Preparing aircraft for the Battle of Britain,
D-Day, Arnhem, Korea, Malaya and so forth.

From the beginning RAF Cosford was planned to house No. 9 MU (Maintenance Unit) as well as the School of Technical Training, which accounts for the ubiquitous turf-covered Lamella storage hangars which are such a prominent feature of the southern side of the airfield. During the war Cosford was full to overflowing with stored aircraft; literally, as two satellite airfields at Weston Park and Brockton had to be built to take the overflow. Dozens of different types of aircraft, and hundreds in number, passed through 9 MU during the war. How I wish some of the staff had broken the law and photographed some of their charges.

A wartime aerial view of Cosford. The airfield is camouflaged with painted 'hedgerows', and the Lamella hangars on the right-hand side are naturally hard to see. The four large workshops on the other side of the railway and the curved row of hangars on the airfield have also been camouflaged, but the effect is rather ruined by the regimented rows of huts and roads in the top left-hand corner. The huge numbers of aircraft scattered about are almost all in store with No. 9 Maintenance Unit.

TYPE.	BALANCE IN STOCK 31.10.40.	RECEIPTS.	TOTAL.	ISSUES.	BALANCE IN STOCK 31.11.40.
ANSON.	16	8	24	11	13
AUDAX.	5	–	5	2	3
AVRO TUTOR.	1	–	1	–	1
BATTLE.	23	29	52	10	42
BLENHEIM. I.	23	–	23	–	23
BLENHEIM. IV.	44	28	72	25	47
BEAUFORT.	3	–	3	–	3
DRAGON RAPIDE.	3	1	4	4	–
DOMINIE.	6	2	8	3	5
FURY.	1	–	1	–	1
HARROW.	3	–	3	–	3
HART.	3	–	3	–	3
HECTOR.	1	–	1	–	1
HIND.	1	2	3	–	3
LYSANDER. I.	1	–	1	–	1
LYSANDER. II.	1	3	4	1	3
LYSANDER. III.	28	15	43	3	40
MAGISTER.	37	1	38	4	34
MOTH CIVILIAN.	2	–	2	–	2
NORTHROP.	13	–	13	2	11
SPITFIRE. I.	15	29	44	13	31
SPITFIRE. II.	5	12	17	6	11
TIGER MOTH.	7	–	7	–	7
WELLINGTON.	32	9	41	11	30
WHITLEY. II.	–	1	1	–	1
WHITLEY. III.	–	2	2	–	2
WHITLEY. V.	5	7	12	6	6
	279	149	428	101	327

An aircraft movement log for No. 9 MU for the month of November 1940, which illustrates the huge variety and number of aircraft handled by the unit. Battles, Blenheims, Lysanders, Magisters and Wellingtons seem to have been the stock-in-trade at the time.

Month	Date	Type	No.	1st Pilot	or Passenger	(Including Results and Remarks
—	—	—	—	—	—	—— Totals Brought Forward
DEC.	17	BLENHEIM IV	KG177	SELF.	—	ASHBOURNE — COSFORD
	20	BEAUFIGHTER VIc	T5323	SELF	—	SHAWBURY — CROSBY —1,1900, 186 K
	20	WELLINGTON III	BK392	SELF	—	DUMFRIES — SQUIRES GATE
	21	WELLINGTON III	BK392	SELF.	—	SQUIRES GATE —29 OTU. N. LUFFENH
		ARGUS I.	HM184	SELF.	HILL.	RATCLIFFE — COSFORD
		BEAUFIGHTER VIc	JL630	SELF	—	COSFORD — LICHFIELD
		ARGUS I.	EV767	SELF.	P/O NICHOLS	LICHFIELD — COSFORD.
		BEAUFIGHTER VIc	JL641	SELF	—	COSFORD — LICHFIELD
		ARGUS I.	EV767	SELF.	PYATT, NICHOLS, MAUNDER	LICHFIELD — COSFORD
	23	WHITLEY V.	LA824	SELF.	F/E CUTHBERT	BAGINTON — ASTON DOWN
		HALIFAX II.	BB264	CAPT: STEDALL	SELF.	L.RISSINGTON — COSFORD
	24	SPITFIRE Vc T.	ES351.	SELF.	—	COSFORD — LICHFIELD
		BEAUFIGHTER VIc	JL575	SELF.	—	LICHFIELD — 236 Sq: NORTH COATES
	28	SPITFIRE Vc T.	ES309	SELF.	—	COSFORD — LICHFIELD
		DOMINIE.	X7255	SELF.	—	COSFORD — HIXON. 125.ASI.
					4 PASS.	HIXON — COSFORD
	29	BEAUFIGHTER VIc	T5332	SELF.	—	COSFORD — LYNEHAM
		BEAUFIGHTER VIf	V8593	SELF.	—	COLERNE — HIGH ERCALL
	30	OXFORD II.	MP545	SELF.	—	ANSTY — RINGWAY.
		WELLINGTON III	BK358	SELF.	—	RINGWAY — 30 OTU. HIXON.
		SPITFIRE Vc T.	ER974.	SELF.	—	COSFORD — HIGH ERCALL.
	31	DEFIANT I.	N3487	SELF	—	COSFORD — PRESTWICK.
		MUSTANG IA.	FD485	SELF.	—	PRESTWICK — LICHFIELD. AS...

GRAND TOTAL [Cols. (1) to (10)]
597   40

Totals Carried Forward

A page from the log-book of Peter Garrod, who was based at Cosford with No. 12
Ferry Pilots' Pool. It illustrates what a tremendous variety of aircraft ferry pilots were
called upon to fly, and the gipsy life they led. Some of the flights were in the unit's
own Fairchild Argus, returning pilots to Cosford or taking them to pick up aircraft
elsewhere.

No. 9 MU had its own Home Guard Unit, and here sixty-eight of them pose for the camera in October 1944.

Defiant TT1 target tug DR972, August 1942. At the time most Defiants were delivered to Cosford, some towed the short distance by road with their outer wings removed. Many of Peter Garrod's deliveries were Defiant target tugs.

"DEFIANT" I.

TRIM TABS FOR TAKE OFF.	1. Elevator	– Zero.
	2. Rudder	– 2½ Starboard.

FLAPS. 25° Down.

AIRSCREW. Lever fully forward, i.e. fully fine pitch.

MIXTURE CONTROL. Right back, i.e. rich.

PETROL COCK. ALL ON.

Fuel Pressure.	2¼ lbs.
Max. Oil T.	90°
Min. Oil P.	60 lbs.
Total fuel	104 gallons.
and oil.	10 gallons.

APPROACH FOR LANDING. Flaps fully down.
Speed 100 m.p.h. I.A.S. MINIMUM.

. . . .

"DEFIANT" II.

MOTOR AIRCRAFT.

AS FOR "DEFIANT" I EXCEPT

TAKE OFF.

1. Rudder Trim, full starboard.

2. Throttle through gate.

3. Supercharger gear change control
in medium, i.e. right out.

EXTRA FUEL DETAILS ISSUED LATER.

The interim ferry pilot's notes for the Defiant Mk. 1 and Mk. II produced by Boulton
Paul Aircraft. Sometimes this was all a ferry pilot had when tackling a new aircraft type.

Members of No. 12 Ferry Pilots' Pool in front of one of their Fairchild Argus taxi aircraft. Back row, left to right: Preston, Collins, Peter Garrod, Bayliss, Mander, Gibbons. Front row: -?-, Death (Operations), Fl. Lt. C. Stedall (CO), Pyatt, Dew.

No. 9 MU stored aircraft at two satellite landing grounds, Brockton and Weston Park, which were camouflaged as completely as possible. This small Robin hangar at Weston Park has been elaborately camouflaged as a country cottage.

No. 9 MU Glider Tug Flight about to erect a Horsa glider from the parts which were made by numerous subcontractors, mostly from the furniture industry, such as Boulton & Paul Ltd, the former parent company of Boulton Paul Aircraft.

After the war the numerous Horsas which had not been left in Normandy or at Arnhem were sold off and found homes as sheds on many farms around Cosford. These two were used into the late 1960s in a timber yard at the entrance to Albrighton station.

Workers of the Glider Tug Flight No. 9 MU during 1944. There are storemen and women, paint sprayers and engineers. They worked primarily on Whitley glider tugs and Horsa gliders. Dorothy Sylvester, now Dorothy Baker, is third from the right on the front row.

The main headquarters building of No. 9 MU in 1949, with the proud gardener standing among his handiwork.

Mr C. Edwards, who was in charge of No. 9 MU's Modifications Office, 1949. In the background is Gwen Saville (now Ryder).

No. 9 MU's Christmas Dinner of 1951 in the canteen. It was followed by the revue *Kristmas Krackers*, produced by R. Sanders, which ended with a rendition of 'Silent Night' by the entire company.

Two 9 MU aircraft at Cosford, around 1950. In the background is a late model Spitfire, and in the foreground is Avro Lincoln B Mk. 2, RA723. Examples of these two aircraft can still be seen at Cosford Aerospace Museum.

Close-up of the nose of Lincoln RA723, with two of 9 MU's engineering staff. This Lincoln was built by Metropolitan-Vickers.

No. 9 MU hangar staff, around 1950.

No. 9 MU office staff inside the headquarters building, around the same time.

Spitfire Mk. 22s at Cosford awaiting a trip to the aluminium smelter, 1955.

More Spitfires in the same group, which was parked by the Lamella hangars on the Albrighton side of the airfield. These are camouflaged Mk. 24s. At the same time there were a number of cocooned Spitfires and three Wellingtons on the other side of the airfield by the top hangars.

Even after No. 9 MU's closure aircraft still come to Cosford for disposal. This Mk. III Shackleton is WR982, one of two with WR974, being dismantled by the RAF in 1988 for the Peter Vallence Collection.

The same hardstanding a little later, and it's a Buccaneer's turn for disposal.

Four

THE BOULTON PAUL CONNECTION

Good relations with friendly neighbours.

RAF Cosford experienced some experimental flying on a few occasions, which was very unusual for a training base. This was due to the proximity of one of the country's major aircraft manufacturers, Boulton Paul Aircraft. Because Cosford had a paved runway, unlike its own airfield at Pendeford, and perhaps because of the greater security, Boulton Paul tested aircraft fitted with secret gun turrets both during and after the war, and then used Cosford's runway for landing tests of its Balliol trainer prototypes, and pre-production aircraft. I have been told that the P111 delta jet also landed at Cosford, but have been unable to confirm this. No. 9 MU stored many Boulton Paul Defiants during the war, most making the short flight from Pendeford; at one stage, however, they were being towed to Cosford with the outer wings removed.

Cosford was used for trials of the Boulton Paul Type D Turret, which was fitted to the tail of a Halifax in 1944. In this picture taken on 10 February the turret is pointing towards the camera but the guns have not been fitted.

Photographed on the same day, the twin 0.5 in Browning machine-guns have now been fitted. Bomber Command had been crying out for turrets with heavy weapons for some time, but the Type D Turret had been delayed by America's entry into the war, and the resultant shortage of 0.5 in guns. In the background are a Wellington and a Lancaster.

This was photographed on 12 February and the turret has now been fitted with AGLT (Airborne Gunlaying for Turrets), the radar scanner being below the turret. Experimental turrets were fitted to Halifaxes at Pendeford normally, but this one may well have been at Cosford because of the secrecy surrounding the radar and the greater security that was possible there.

Avro Lancaster LL780/G at Cosford, 2 December 1946. It is fitted with Boulton Paul remote-controlled cannon barbettes in dorsal and ventral positions, though the twin 20 mm cannon are not installed. The G suffix to the serial is a wartime indication that the aircraft should be guarded at all times when on the ground. The aircraft behind is a Mosquito.

The upper barbette with the cupola removed to show the twin cannon. This was taken in February 1944, when the Lancaster was first fitted with the system.

Another view of the cannon barbettes on LL780/G. They were electrically controlled and the gunner's sighting position was in the tail.

The 'DF' codes of the Lancaster were for the Central Bomber Establishment. This weapon system was abandoned and the RAF never fitted defensive armament to its new jet bombers, unlike the Soviet Union or America.

Balliol T2 pre-production aircraft VR596, which undertook landing trials at Cosford.

Boulton Paul pre-production aircraft VR603, with Cosford's runway just visible above the port roundel. In July 1952, on an air test from Pendeford, this aircraft suffered a starboard undercarriage collapse while landing at Cosford, damaging the wing.

A Boulton Paul Type D Turret on display in the tail of the Aerospace Museum's Avro Lincoln. Compare this with the Halifax's turret on page 69.

A group of Dowty Boulton Paul employees, standing in front of the Boulton Paul Sea Balliol, donating to the Aerospace Museum two Dowty Boulton Paul power-flying controls and a model of a VC10 in which they were fitted. Left to right: R. Tipper, Bill Cook, M. Tandy, Jack Chambers, unknown museum assistant, E. Albrecht, N. Webb, Derek Eastwood (museum curator), A.J. Morgan, D. Roberts, D. Hammond, F. Hewitt, J. Holmes, -?-, N. Stewart, R. Fellows, L. Tongue, D. Moutney, R. Cutler.

Boulton Paul Sea Balliol T21, WL732, on display in the Aerospace Museum's experimental hangar, one of only five Boulton Paul-designed aircraft left in the world and preserved fittingly close to its birthplace.

Five

THE AEROSPACE
MUSEUM

*Inspiring and informing the young, and reminding
the old.*

The Aerospace Museum is an outstation of the Royal Air Force Museum, and includes aircraft of the RAF Museum's reserve collection and the British Airways collection of airliners. It is undoubtedly one of the finest aircraft museums in the world, as well as one of the largest. It displays a very high proportion of absolutely unique aircraft, particularly in its collection of Second World War Axis aircraft and British experimental aircraft. The job done by its small number of permanent staff and the stalwarts of its volunteers is outstanding.

Aerial view of part of the Aerospace Museum site in the early 1980s. The museum aircraft are, from left to right: VC10 (G-ARVM), Short Belfast C1 (XR371), Boeing 707–436 (G-APFJ), Hastings T5 (TG511), Vulcan B2 (XM598), Lockheed Neptune (204), Trident 1 (G-ARPH). Behind the 707 are four Folland Gnat trainers, of the Airfield Training Flight, two in Red Arrows colours.

The unique Kawasaki Ki.100-1b, one of the best Japanese fighters of the last war, is seen here in the 1960s in an entirely spurious colour scheme.

Vickers Viscount 701 G-AMOG, part of the Aerospace Museum's British Airways airliner collection. It is shown here in British Airways colours, as it was when it first arrived, before being repainted in BEA colours.

The Avro Lincoln B2, RF398, in the museum's upper hangar, with a 10-ton bomb nestling beneath it. This aircraft is reputed to be haunted.

The Supermarine 517 experimental aircraft, VV106, is now no longer at the Aerospace Museum. Being basically an all-swept Supermarine Attacker, it was transferred to the Fleet Air Arm Collection and now resides at Lee-on-Solent.

The magnificent TSR2, XR220, pictured in 1982, fifteen years after its tragic cancellation. The museum has since been extensively re-arranged, and this aircraft now dominates a hangar full of experimental jets. The Vickers Viking in the background has gone to Brooklands, though the Fairey Gyrodyne helicopter remains at Cosford.

An historic Hawker Hunter, WT555, outside the museum's upper hangars. This was the first production F1, first flying on 16 May 1953. It was originally built without the large air-brake which can be seen extended beneath the fuselage. Early Hunters had them retrofitted.

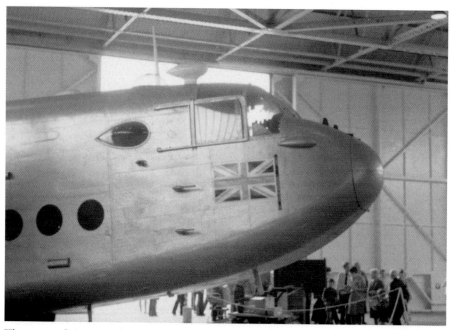

The nose of Avro York, TS798, which was built after the war for joint RAF/BOAC services. It is therefore probably the most appropriate exhibit in a museum which features both RAF transports and British Airways airliners.

Avro Vulcan B1 XA900, ex-101 Squadron and instructional airframe 7896M, in its nuclear-bomber all-white scheme. This aircraft was broken up in the mid-1970s because of corrosion and was replaced in the museum by a Vulcan B2.

A truly historic aircraft, which is no longer at Cosford, is the Hunter F3, WB188, in which Neville Duke broke the world's absolute Air Speed Record. This aircraft is now on loan to the Tangmere Aircraft Museum.

De Havilland Comet IXB, ex-Air France F-BGNZ, in the colours of BOAC's G-APAS, flanking the entrance to the British Airways Exhibition with Viscount G-AMOG.

Boeing 707–436, G-APFJ, an ex-BOAC aircraft but in British Airtours colours.

Venom FB4, J-1704, of the Swiss Air Force. It is standing behind the museum's upper hangars, but looks almost as if it could be at dispersal on a Swiss air base. The Venom is one of a number of foreign aircraft at Cosford presented to the RAF Museum by their former owners.

The newly arrived Lockheed Neptune '204' of the Dutch Navy, October 1982. The aircraft is still on the airfield side of the wire, outside the museum compound.

The Aerospace Museum curator, Derek Eastwood, receives the log-books of Vulcan B2, XM598, from the crew who had just flown it into Cosford, January 1983. The Station Commander, Group Captain Morgan, is on the right.

The newly repainted De Havilland Devon C2/2, VP952, which forms part of the museum's transport collection.

Lockheed T-33A, 17472, ex-French Air Force, behind the museum's top hangars. Never put on display as such, it has now been loaned to the Midland Air Museum, Coventry, who plan to convert it to a single-seat P80.

A relic of the Falklands War: a wrecked FMA IA 58A Pucara attack aircraft of the Argentinian Air Force, serial A-528, captured at Stanley Airport. This Pucara has now been passed on to the Museum of Army Flying at Middle Wallop.

The Aerospace Museum's 'new' Argentinian Pucara, A-515 (also captured at Stanley Airport), on the day it was flown in, after flight trials at Boscombe Down.

The centre-piece of one of the museum's regular special Exhibitions, 'Boulton (&) Paul Aircraft Since 1915', this is the Sea Balliol WL732, the nose of which is flanked by Merlin and Mamba engines. The second prototype Balliol T1 was the world's first aircraft powered by a single turbo-prop, but production Balliols were powered by the Merlin – the last Merlin-powered aircraft built in this country.

The most historic part of the exhibition, the oldest British metal aircraft wing in existence, is the wing of the Boulton & Paul P10, built in 1919.

The P10 wing was the oldest piece of Boulton & Paul aircraft structure on display; this was the youngest, the tailplane of the last Boulton Paul design to fly, the P120 delta wing research aircraft – a test specimen only because the aircraft crashed on Salisbury Plain.

On a rare outing from the Museum into the fresh air for an Air Show, Meteor NF.14, WS843, representing the last incarnation of the Meteor line, which began with the prototype seen below.

The prototype Meteor, DG202/G, perhaps the most historic aircraft in the whole exhibition. The Meteor was the first jet aircraft in the world to enter operational service.

Part of the Aerospace Museum's unique collection of Second World War German missiles: in the foreground the V-1 flying bomb, behind it the V-2 rocket, to the right the Enzian and Rheintochter 1 remote-controlled anti-aircraft rockets.

Two absolutely unique Japanese wartime aircraft. In the background is the beautifully restored Mitsubishi Ki.46 'Dinah', and the tail of the Ki.100b fighter now restored to its correct wartime markings.

A replica of the Moon buggy which was on display in the Museum for many years. It was one of the few exhibits which justified the 'space' suffix to the title Aerospace Museum.

An unusual RAF aircraft, an Auster C.4, WE600, which had taken part in a Trans-Antarctic Expedition in the 1950s, when it would have worn skis.

One of the later additions to the British Airways collection at Cosford, the BAC.111-510 ED, G-AVMO, which, with the demise of the British Airways Collection, was gifted to the Museum of Flight at East Fortune.

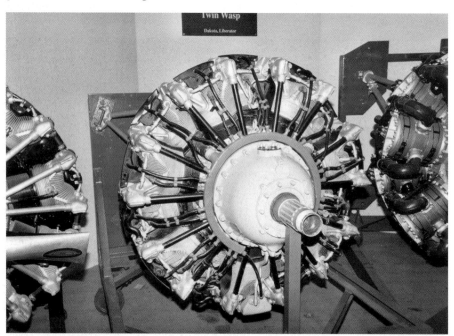

The museum has always had an extensive collection of engines on display, and this is a Pratt & Whitney Twin Wasp, showing the immaculate condition in which they are displayed.

The new Michael Beetham Conservation Centre became the centre for the RAF Museum's restoration, and was to prepare a number of aircraft for the Milestone's of Flight Gallery at Hendon, including the Hawker Tempest V, which was to be finished in target tug markings.

Another restoration bound for the Milestone's of Flight gallery was this Miles Mohawk, which had been built to the order of Charles Lindbergh.

A longer term restoration, which will take many years, is this Handley Page Hampden, P1344, recovered from its crash site in Russia. It will be restored on one side only, showing the history of its exposure to the elements on the other side.

Hawker Hart Trainer, K4972, which was on display at Cosford for many years, but after refurbishment in the Michael Beetham Centre, shown here, was then transferred to Hendon.

Six

THE INDOOR ATHLETICS ARENA

And some can fly without wings.

For many years Cosford was most well known to the general public as the home of British Indoor Athletics, although it may be fading a little from the public mind lately, since the construction of the National Indoor Arena and others. I have often wondered how many international athletes stepped down from a train at the tiny wooden platform of Cosford station, looked around for the Indoor Athletics Arena, and decided there must be some other place called Cosford. Yet, with its central location, with its own airfield, its own railway station, and the M54 motorway only half a mile away, could there be a better location for a national sports venue?

A general view of the Indoor Athletics Stadium at Cosford as it first looked in the mid-1960s, at the start of a 60 m race. The building began life as No. 4 Workshop.

Looking the other way during a different 60 m race, this photograph shows the sparsely populated spectators' seating and the original wooden track, which was later replaced by a permanent concrete structure.

Ralph Banthorpe winning the 200 m in 1970. Improvements to the track have been made, not least the outside rail.

Roger Waters of Wolverhampton & Bilston Athletic Club winning a 220 yard race in 1967. Having the country's only indoor arena just down the road was an undoubted advantage for the local club.

Gwynne Griffiths of Wolverhampton & Bilston Athletic Club winning the AAA 400 m Championship in 1970.

The AAA Junior 440 yard Championship, 17 December 1966. Some runners adapt well to the tight bends of indoor running; Ralph Banthorpe, depicted here, was one of those who revelled in the new indoor arena. He ran a faster time than the Senior race, in which he had not been allowed to compete because he was too young.

RAF Cosford's own Don Halliday losing a 60 m race in the 1960s by committing the cardinal sin for a sprinter of looking sideways at the finishing line.

The winning Wolverhampton & Bilston 100 m relay team at the AAA Indoor Championships, March 1968. Left to right: Gwynne Griffiths, Alan Jones, Charles Taylor (Club Chairman), Ralph Banthorpe, Roger Waters.

The finish of the 400 m in an international match against East Germany. Muller, No. 3, is winning, Gwynne Griffiths, No. 2, is coming second, Taylor (partially hidden) is third, and Ebert fourth.

The Junior 220 yard race in the AAA Indoor Championship of 1967, with Ralph Banthorpe, the eventual winner, on the inside. The 200 m races are now run in lanes indoors. From the battle going on here at the first bend it is easy to see why the change was made.

The finish of the 60 m sprint in a women's international match against East Germany. Left to right: Sonia Lannaman, Christina Brehmer, and the winner Andrea Lynch.

One of the greatest of Britain's women athletes, Verona Bernard (later Verona Elder), winning the 400 m in an international match at Cosford against Belgium. She was to represent her country more times than any other woman.

An international match against West Germany, February 1985. Todd Bennet leads the 400 m runners round the banking on the new tartan surface.

Some false starts are more obvious than others. This lady is well on the way to finishing the 60 m, before the gun.

The great pole-vaulter Serge Bubka carrying his pole back down the runway. The magnificent mural in the background was painted by a prisoner from Featherstone Prison. There was a delay in its completion when he escaped for a while!

Bubka clears the bar. He has broken the World Record so many times since 1985 that the relatively low roof at Cosford would seem to preclude any further attempts there. The hangar was not built with pole-vaulters in mind, at least not those of his ability.

Charles Taylor with the great Czech 400 m/800 m runner Jarmila Kratchvilova. He is holding on to her because she had arrived in the country without a visa, and was only permitted entry in his custody!

Seven

OPEN DAYS AND AIR DISPLAYS

A chance to get close to the aircraft.

The annual Cosford Air Day, for many years one of the RAF's Battle of Britain Open Days usually held in September, has more recently had a regular date in June, and become a major fund-raising venture for the Aerospace Museum. It is a day when people from Shropshire and the Black Country flock to Cosford to enjoy the world of aviation; and a day when there are a little more than gliders and Bulldogs in the skies over Cosford.

No. 2 SCHOOL OF TECHNICAL TRAINING (APPRENTICES).

R.A.F. STATION, COSFORD.

1st Parents' Day
July 15th, 1939.

FLYING DISPLAY
(Weather Permitting).

By kind permission of Group Captain W. J. Y. GUILFOYLE, O.B.E., M.C.
Officer in charge of flying: Wing Commander J. OLIVER, A.F.C.

NOTES.

No cameras are allowed.

Please keep behind all ropes.

Smoking near aircraft is not allowed.

Do not encroach on the landing ground—it endangers the lives of aircraft crews and your own.

The Air Ministry will not hold themselves responsible for loss or damage to individuals through any cause whatsoever, and this is an express condition of entry to aerodrome.

Buses run between camp and aerodrome every 5 minutes—Fare 1d.

We are indebted to the Officer Commanding and Officers of Nos. 5 & 10 F.T.S. and No. 9 Maintenance Unit for their assistance in the Flying Programme.

——:——

During the Display it is hoped to show " The Cosford Special." This is a Hush-Hush Plane on the Air Ministry Secret List and permission to allow it to take the air has been refused. The aircraft may taxy round the enclosure.

——:——

Any urgent messages for broadcasting may be handed to the Duty Pilot in the Watch Office (square-towered building on Aerodrome).

For List of Events see over.

PROGRAMME OF EVENTS

Event 1
From 4 p.m.

EXHIBITION OF AIRCRAFT.

Aircraft are arranged in the Old Type Park (first on entering) and the New Type Park.
This will show progress in design in recent years.
Numbers displayed by aircraft correspond to the following :—

OLD TYPE PARK :

1.	HART :	Light Bomber.
2.	D.H. MOTH :	Light Trainer.
3.	GORDON :	Medium Bomber and Reconnaisance.
4.	LYNX AVRO :	Trainer. The forerunner of this type was produced prior to 1914 and revolutionized flying instruction.
5.	FURY :	Single Seater Fighter.
6.	GAUNTLET :	Single Seater Fighter.
7.	HEYFORD :	Heavy Bomber.

NEW TYPE PARK.

8.	MENTOR :	Communication Aircraft.
9.	HARVARD :	American Trainer.
10.	MAGISTER :	Light Trainer.
11.	LYSANDER :	Army Co-operation.
12.	DON :	Communication Aircraft.
13.	BATTLE :	Light Bomber.
14.	OXFORD :	Twin-Engine Trainer.
15.	ANSON :	General Reconnaisance.
16.	BLENHEIM :	Medium Bomber.
17.	HUDSON :	American Bomber.
18.	HARROW :	Heavy Bomber.
19.	SPITFIRE :	Single Seater Fighter.

Airmen are stationed at Aircraft to answer simple questions. It is forbidden to enter Aircraft.

Event 2.
5.15 p.m.

AIR DRILL DISPLAY : By 5 Harvard Aircraft of No. 5 F.T.S. Aircraft will appear over Aerodrome and after various evolutions will return to Tern Hill without landing. This type of Aircraft is available for inspection in New Type Park (No. 9).

Event 3.
5.30 p.m.

INDIVIDUAL AEROBATICS : By Single Seater Fighter Aircraft, demonstrating loops, half rolls, rolls, roll off-loop, spin, upside-down flying, etc.

Event 4.
5.45 p.m.

PARENTS FLYING COMPETITION : In which three parents (two fathers and one mother) of apprentices have volunteered to attempt to fly solo for the first time. This event will be broadcast by our special commentator.

Event 5.
6 p.m.

DISPLAY OF HIGH SPEED FLYING : By single modern type fighter aircraft.

Event 6.
6.10 p.m.

FLY PAST BY TYPES : Aircraft will take off, fly past and land in the following order.
MAGISTER — HART — MENTOR — ANSON
OXFORD — FURY — HARVARD — GAUNTLET

The End.

The programme of events for the first Open Day at Cosford, a Parents' Day in 1939.

The Red Arrows making their usual entrance from behind the crowd, a regular feature of Cosford Air Days in more recent times.

ROYAL AIR FORCE STATION · COSFORD ·

SEUL LE PREMIER PAS COUTE

Battle of Britain

"At Home Day"

SATURDAY, SEPTEMBER 16th, 1950

After the war the early air displays at Cosford were usually Battle of Britain Days, held in September, when numerous stations all over the country would be open. This programme is interesting because it features the Cosford crest.

Percival Prentice, VS281, at the 1956 air display.

Vampire Mk. 5, WX201, taxiing past the crowd during the same display.

R.A.F. COSFORD

At Home

SATURDAY 15th SEPTEMBER 1951

in Commemoration of the

Battle of Britain

All Proceeds in Aid of Royal Air Force Charities

Admission Free   Souvenir Programme 1/-

The cover of the programme for the 1951 display. It is interesting to see that admission was free, and the programme only cost a shilling. Prices have gone up just slightly since then!

Percival Provost, WV506, one of seven Provosts to appear in the 1956 display.

The entrance to No. 9 MU's fun-fair, 1951. It was located in the second of the large C-type hangars, with the first given over to refreshments.

Some of the senior station officers quite happily throwing away their money. There is a late model, Griffon-engined Spitfire in the background.

Another of the side-shows at the fun-fair, with the photographer being encouraged to try his hand with the darts. The lady on the right is Gwen Saville, the others are unknown.

The essence of air displays: small boys, with rucksacks on their backs, staring in wonder at the aircraft. Though this Harvard, FT375, and the USAF C-47 behind are Second World War aircraft, this picture was taken at the 1963 display.

A rather savage-looking Hunter, 8002M, one of the station's instructional airframes, 1963.

A Gloster Javelin, XA899, presumably an instructional airframe, although retaining its operational serial. It is unusual in having a white radome.

Piper Aztec, G-ARYF, hired by the *Evening Mail* to transport pictures of the 1963 Battle of Britain Display.

Avro Lincoln, RF398, on one of its rare visits to the sunlight at a Battle of Britain Display, 1960s.

The next generation of Avro bomber, a Vulcan B2, with another behind, and a Victor also visible in the hangar. They were all in use as instructional airframes at the time.

The weather in 1963 was clearly cold judging by the coats and scarves in evidence, but the sun is glinting on the nose of this Twin Pioneer, ideal weather for the flying display.

NORTH WEST AIR SERVICES

MANCHESTER AIRPORT
WYTHENSHAWE, MANCHESTER, 22.

12/6

FLIGHT TICKET

A ticket for a flight in a De Havilland DH–83C Fox Moth, G-AOJH, at the 1959 Battle of Britain Day at Cosford. With this, bought for the princely sum of *12s 6d*, the author enjoyed his first flight.

An unusual view down Cosford's runway of the Boeing B–17, 'Sally B', taking part in the 1988 Air Day.

The Goodyear airship *Europa* visiting Cosford during the 1980s.

The Falcons Parachute Display Team, always a popular part of any air display, are in the air over Cosford.

The World Land Speed Record Holder, Richard Noble's Thrust 2, Cosford, 1984. Powered by an Avon jet engine this car achieved 633.468 mph on 4 October 1983.

A Pitts S2A Special of the Marlboro Display Team at the 1981 display. The reason the lettering is upside down is explained below.

The team operated as a mirror-image pair, flying their manoeuvres head to head, as it were.

A Stampe SV4C, G-ATIR, in the 1981 display. The spectators on top of the distant Lamella hangar are getting one of the best views available of the display.

One of the more unusual items seen in a Cosford air display is this Pilatus P2 trainer, formerly of the Swiss Air Force, being flown by Mark Hanna, 1983.

Aircraft of the Battle of Britain Memorial Flight: Spitfire, Lancaster and Hurricane. An essential part of any Cosford display.

An Avro Vulcan in the air, performing a touch and go at the 1981 display. A magnificent sight which will be seen no more.

The almost unknown residents of RAF Cosford are Bob Mitchell's fleet of Second World War trainers. They are usually kept in the Aerospace Museum's storage hangar, one of the Lamellas, which also contains other unseen delights, including an unrestored Fairey Swordfish, a Lockheed Ventura, and a Fairchild Argus. The centre aircraft here is his Vultee Valiant.

The dreadfully noisy Harvard Display Team: a C45 leads a gaggle of North American Harvards (Texans), one of which had been rebuilt as a single-seater to imitate a Japanese Zero for the film *Tora Tora Tora*.

The YAK–5OP aircraft, one of many which have been brought to this country, at the 1994 display.

The beautiful Dragon Rapide, G-AIDL, of Caernarfon Air, also at the 1994 display.

Visiting aircraft at the 1994 display.

The P47 Thunderbolt of The Fighter Collection, evidence of the Air Show 'industry' which enables exotic aircraft to be bought and restored because people just love to see them in the air, and will pay handsomely to do so. However, those gathered on Albrighton Bowling Club in the background paid more modestly.

A single Hawk of the Red Arrows, silhouetted against a setting sun at the end of the 1984 display, makes a fitting finale.

Acknowledgements

Many individuals and organizations have helped me with photographs for this book, either lending them, or guiding me to people who had them. I am grateful to all of them, and I apologize if there is anyone missing from the following list:

Bill Aldridge • Roy Ashby • Dorothy Baker • Boulton Paul Association
Peter Brew • Jack Chambers • Dowty Boulton Paul Ltd • John Francis
Peter Garrod • J.B. Gray • Cyril Harper • Sgt. A. Joyner • A.M. Kennedy
Stephen King • Peter Lancaster • R.J. McAlpine • M.J. Pheasant
RAF Air Historical Branch • RAF Museum • Gwen Ryder • Keith Sedgewick
Sqd. Ldr. Sherwood-Moore • A.J. Spilsbury • Charles Taylor • N.D. Welch.

This looks for all the World like a collection of model aircraft, but is in fact a collection of the types used by No. 60 Squadron. Most of them are Museum aircraft, augmented by the Bristol Blenheim of the Aircraft Restoration Company, two replica SE.5As and a Bell Griffin, the current equipment of No. 60 Squadron at nearby RAF Shawbury.